D0615316

School Survival

Keeping Your Cool at School

ABDO
Publishing Company

Strong, Beautiful Girls

School
Survival

Keeping Your Cool at School

by Tina Gagliardi

Content Consultant
Vicki F. Panaccione, PhD
Licensed Child Psychologist
Founder, Better Parenting Institute

Credits

Published by ABDO Publishing Company, 8000 West 78th Street, Edina, Minnesota 55439. Copyright © 2009 by Abdo Consulting Group, Inc. International copyrights reserved in all countries. No part of this book may be reproduced in any form without written permission from the publisher. The Essential Library™ is a trademark and logo of ABDO Publishing Company.

Printed in the United States.

Special thanks to Dr. Vicki Panaccione for her expertise and guidance in shaping this series.

Editor: Erika Wittekind
Copy Editor: Patricia Stockland
Interior Design and Production: Becky Daum
Cover Design: Becky Daum

Library of Congress Cataloging-in-Publication Data
Gagliardi, Tina.
  School survival : keeping your cool at school / by Tina Gagliardi.
    p. cm. — (Essential health : strong, beautiful girls)
  Includes index.
  ISBN 978-1-60453-104-6
  1. Schoolgirls—Life skills guides—Juvenile literature. 2. Teenage girls—Education—Social aspects—Juvenile literature. I. Title.

LC1481.G34 2008
373.18—dc22
                              2008011904

Contents

eet Dr. Vicki

Throughout the series Strong, Beautiful Girls, you'll hear the reassuring, knowledgeable voice of Dr. Vicki Panaccione, a licensed psychologist with more than 25 years of experience working with teens, children, and families. Dr. Vicki offers her expert advice to girls who find themselves in the difficult situations described in each chapter.

Better known as the Parenting Professor™, Dr. Vicki is founder of the Better Parenting Institute™ and author of *Discover Your Child* and *What Your Kids Would Tell You . . . If Only You'd Ask!* You might have seen her name quoted in publications such as the *New York Times*, *Family Circle*, and *Parents* magazine.

While her credentials run deep, perhaps what qualifies her most to advise girls on everything from body image to friendship to schoolwork is that she's been there, so she can relate. "I started out in junior high as the chubby new kid with glasses and freckles, who the popular kids loved to tease or even worse . . . ignore," says the doc. "They should see me now!"

Today, Dr. Vicki maintains a private practice in Melbourne, Florida, and writes articles for a variety of periodicals and Web sites. She has been interviewed or quoted in major publications including *Parenting* magazine, *Reader's Digest*, *First for Women*, and *Woman's World*, networks such as Fox, ABC, NBC, and CBS, and several popular Web sites. Dr. Vicki joined esteemed colleagues Tony Robbins, Dr. Wayne Dyer, and Bill Bartmann as coauthor of *The Power of Team*, the latest in the best-selling series Wake Up and Live the Life You Love. She is an adviser for the Web site parentalwisdom.com and also for MTV/Nickelodeon's parentsconnect.com. She is a clinical consultant for Red Line Editorial, Inc. Not to mention, she's the proud mother of Alex, her 21-year-old son who is pursuing his PhD to become a medical researcher.

With all that she has going for her now, it might be hard to imagine that Dr. Vicki was ever an awkward teen struggling to find her way. But consider this—she's living proof that no matter how bleak things might look now, they do get better. The following stories and Dr. Vicki's guidance will help you discover your own path to happiness and success, becoming the Strong, Beautiful Girl you are meant to be.

Take It from Me

During my adolescence, I was not always the best student. In grade school, I did well in all my classes, but by the time I started seventh grade, something had changed. Although I was doing better than some of my classmates in art, music, and English, I began to fall behind in math and science. I felt like something was wrong with me and that I had suddenly become less smart, but I didn't know why. I became less interested in academics, even the subjects I'd enjoyed before. I started to choose seats at the very back of the classroom to avoid participating. At home, I read all the time, but I would skip doing the assigned reading.

Later on, my parents had me switch schools in the hope that I would do better somewhere else. I didn't. Adjusting to a new environment with all new people seemed to make things worse. Eventually, I agreed to get a tutor for math and science. To my surprise, with some extra help, I was able to do well in the subjects that had been difficult for me before. It wasn't easy, but once I applied myself and got the help I needed, I caught up and stayed on track.

If I could go back now and talk to the girl I was then, I would explain that everyone has different strengths and weaknesses. I would tell myself to put extra effort into the subjects

that I did well in, because years later I would discover that they hinted at what talents I have.

As we grow older, our individual strengths
and talents begin to emerge. At the same time,
we may struggle with some parts of school
that had come easily before. Very few students
excel in everything. Even girls who do well in
their academic classes may feel insecure about
other areas, such as athletics or art. Some may
do well on assignments but struggle under the
pressure of taking tests. Others may be good
students but have trouble fitting in with their
peers.

As we move through the school years, it
seems like everything gets more complicated.
Everyone faces obstacles as they get older.
This is part of the challenge of growing into
ourselves as unique individuals. This book shares
the experiences of girls just like you who have
all faced their own challenges in school. I hope
that reading about their growing pains will help
you survive—and thrive—through the challeng-
ing years ahead.

XOXO,
Tina

1

The Worry Wart

No one likes tests, but for some girls, the pressure of exam day is almost too much to take. Some students who work hard to succeed in school have overly high expectations about the grades they'll get. Others lack confidence in their own abilities and feel overwhelmed under the pressure of taking tests. Although they are prepared for an exam, as soon as they walk into the classroom they become very nervous, and in some cases their minds may even go blank. The more nervous these students get, the less they are able to concentrate or recall what they studied.

In either case, these girls may have symptoms such as dry mouth, stomachache, sweating, dizziness, faster heartbeat, and nausea. They may feel confused, scared, and isolated. Maybe they think that there is

The more nervous these students get, the less they are able to concentrate or recall what they studied.

something wrong with them or that they are the only one with this problem. Their embarrassment may cause them to make up a reason for why they did poorly.

Mai is one girl who studied hard but still couldn't take the pressure of test day. Take a look at Mai's story to see how she dealt with test-taking anxiety.

Mai's Story

Mai and Rachel were best friends. Both girls liked school and got good grades. They were in the same history class and had a big test coming up. Mai was a little bit nervous about the test. Memorizing names and dates was difficult for her. She had always been better at problem solving and explaining events. Rachel, on the other hand, seemed to have an easier time with memorization.

Mai and Rachel decided to study for the test together. They met up at Rachel's house every day after school for four days before the test. They took turns quizzing each other, and by the fourth day they really knew the material. However, on the night before the test, Mai told Rachel she was going to look over her notes one more time before she went to bed. Rachel felt she had prepared enough. She chose to take the rest of the night off from studying.

Talk About It

- **Why do you think Mai decided to study more the night before the test while Rachel chose to take the night off?**

- **Does studying with a friend make it easier for you to prepare for tests?**

- **Do you find that some things are easier for you to learn than others?**

- **Do you study differently for different subjects or different kinds of tests?**

Mai's parents put a lot of emphasis on education and expected her to get good grades. They always checked her homework to make sure she'd finished everything. They offered help if she was unsure about an answer or stuck on an assignment. Mai also put pressure on herself to do well. She had a history of high marks and wanted to succeed in school so that she could get into a good college eventually.

The night before the test, Mai had trouble sleeping because she was worried about how she would do.

Her stomach was so upset in the morning that she couldn't eat any breakfast, so she took the time to look over her notes instead. She was glad that her history test was first thing in the morning. She could get it over with quickly, while the material she studied was still fresh in her mind.

Talk About It

- Have you ever felt nervous or worried before a test?

- Have you ever felt pressured by your parents to get good grades? Were their expectations realistic or too demanding?

- What advice would you give Mai before her test?

That morning, as her teacher began handing out the tests, Mai started to feel sick. She had butterflies in her stomach, and her palms were sweaty. The test was made up of multiple-choice questions. Each presented an event and gave three or four options for dates and names that matched the event. As Mai looked down at the paper in front of her, she felt dizzy and wanted to throw up. She struggled to read the first question, but it barely made sense to her. She looked at the answer options and had no idea which one was right. She read the question again.

As Mai looked down at the paper in front of her, she felt dizzy and wanted to throw up. She struggled to read the first question, but it barely made sense to her.

She knew it was something that Rachel had quizzed her on, but she just kept drawing a blank.

Mai looked up at the clock and saw that ten minutes had already passed. She decided to skip the first question and move on. But when she started reading the next question, she had the same reaction. Each multiple-choice option seemed like it could be the right answer. Mai looked up at the clock again. She was running out of time to finish and still hadn't answered a single question. With only five minutes left before the test was over, Mai decided to pick random answers, even though she knew they were probably wrong. Feeling frantic and embarrassed, Mai finished circling her answers just seconds before her time was up. Her teacher asked the students to pass their exams to the person next to them. That person would grade the test while she read the correct answers out loud.

Talk About It

- **Why do you think Mai felt sick when she started her test? Have you ever felt sick or anxious during an exam?**

- **Why did Mai have trouble understanding the questions on the test?**

- **Have you ever drawn a blank during test time, even though you knew the answers when you were studying? What did you do about it?**

Now that the test was over, Mai felt more relaxed. As she graded her classmate's paper, every answer seemed clear to her. Some of the multiple-choice options were so far off from the real answer that they would have been easy to eliminate. Mai couldn't understand why the answers came to her so easily now. When Mai got her test back, she saw that she had failed. She was embarrassed to turn her exam in to the teacher. She figured her teacher would think she hadn't studied. Even though she was ashamed about failing, she decided to talk to her teacher after class and explain what had happened.

Talk About It

- **Why did Mai know the answers when the test was over?**

- **Have you ever talked to your teacher about your grades or another problem? What happened?**

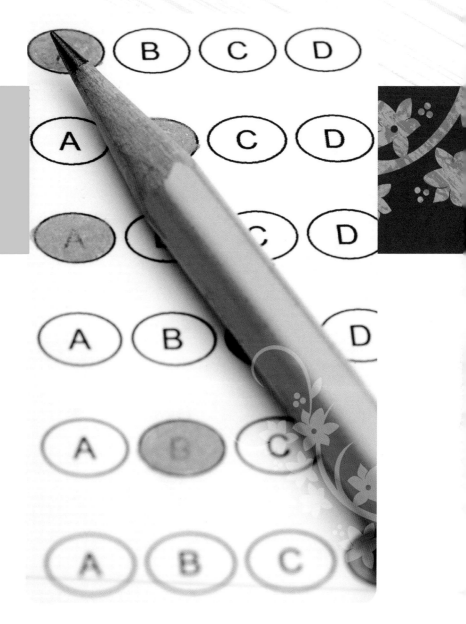

Some of the symptoms of test anxiety can be very scary. The symptoms themselves can lead to more anxiety and even less ability to concentrate on the test. If a student freezes and ends up doing poorly, she may feel even more stressed about the next test.

Girls in Mai's situation would benefit from learning ways to relax at test time. Mai's anxiety was triggered by the fact that she was overly focused on the idea that she might not do well. Girls who are well prepared for exams do better when they walk into the classroom thinking, "I will do well on this test because I know the material."

Get Healthy

1. Talk to an adult you trust about the anxiety you feel when taking tests. The more you keep your problem to yourself, the more you will keep worrying. If you feel your parents are putting too much pressure on you, talk to them about it. You also could have your teacher or guidance counselor set up a meeting with your parents to bring up the issues of stress and pressure.

2. Some schools allow you to take practice tests, which can help ease panic at exam time. Some teachers also allow oral tests

in place of written tests for students who suffer from test anxiety. Ask your teacher what options might be available.

3. Have your parents quiz you or help you make up practice tests. This should decrease the pressure when it's time for the real thing. Practice taking the kinds of tests your teacher gives, whether they're essay, multiple-choice, matching, or fill-in-the-blank.

4. Learn ways to relax. Simple techniques such as taking deep breaths or counting backward slowly from ten can help lessen anxiety.

The Last Word from Tina

Many girls experience test anxiety, even when they enter the classroom feeling well prepared. Overcoming your fear frees you so you can do your best. Many schools have options available to help students who suffer from test anxiety. Telling a parent, teacher, or guidance counselor that you are having a problem is the first step to finding a solution. They can help you learn techniques to stay calm when anxiety starts to rise. Learning how to cope with stress is an important skill that you will be able to use in all kinds of situations, not just when taking tests.

2
The Star Student

It may seem like overachievers have it easy because they do well in school while juggling a number of sports and activities. In reality, doing it all can be difficult. These students may feel overwhelmed and overextended. They have a tendency to join everything instead of choosing a few priority activities on which to focus their energies.

Additionally, these girls may feel pressure to keep matching past achievements with new goals, even when the demands become unreasonable. Results that don't live up to their lofty expectations can lower their self-esteem.

As students climb through the grade levels, both schoolwork and activities demand more time. Girls who take on too much begin to struggle with balancing everything. Striving to achieve success in school and wanting to participate in extracurricular activities are positive goals. But taking on more than one person can handle can lead to negative results. A student's grades may drop, or she may not perform as well in some activities that demand a big time commitment.

Lauren had many interests but soon realized that she was spreading herself too thin. She ended up having to take a hard look at her priorities.

Lauren's Story

Lauren had always done well in school and brought home straight As on her report card. Succeeding in school was something that seemed to come naturally to her from an early age. She had a number of interests outside her studies, as well. In elementary school she made friends by joining the county rec leagues for basketball and soccer. She also performed in the school play each year. As she got older, she even had the lead part a few times.

Girls who take on too much begin to struggle with balancing everything.

Her parents encouraged her participation in extracurricular activities and praised her for getting good

grades. Lauren loved the recognition she got for getting As, playing well in a game, or performing onstage. She felt a sense of pride knowing that she had worked hard and it had paid off. She also liked being busy and couldn't imagine giving anything up. However as Lauren got older, it became more difficult to manage all of her commitments.

When Lauren started junior high, she was excited to try out for the basketball team. Even though this team required more practices than the rec league, she liked the idea of being able to represent her school. At the same time, Lauren's teachers began giving more homework. The material was more difficult, so she found she had to study more to do well on exams. Still, when auditions for the school play came up, Lauren was eager to sign up. She was thrilled when she got one of the lead roles. Then she realized that this play was longer than anything she'd been in before. She would need to put in a lot of time rehearsing and memorizing lines. She figured she could study a little less and not do any extra-credit assignments.

Although she thought she would be able to handle it all, she started feeling the crunch. Between play rehearsals and basketball practices, she had less time to do her schoolwork. She used to enjoy schoolwork, but studying became less enjoyable for Lauren because now she felt like she was always rushing to get things done.

Talk About It

- Why did Lauren no longer enjoy studying? Has this ever happened to you?

- Has participating in an extracurricular activity ever made it more difficult for you to find time to study?

As Lauren got further into the basketball season, practices were longer, and she started coming home even later. She got so tired that she was having trouble focusing on the court. She made stupid mistakes during games and then got down on herself afterward. Lauren tried going over her lines for the play on the bus to away games while her teammates spent the rides joking around. It was too loud to concentrate, and she wished she could just relax like everyone else.

Meanwhile, she began to put off studying for tests until the night before and skipped a few homework assignments completely. Since schoolwork had always come easily to her, she assumed she still would get pretty good grades. Lauren had a history test coming up and decided that she knew the material well enough, so she skipped reviewing it. Even though she hadn't studied, she was shocked when her test came back the next day with a big fat D. The low grade worried Lauren, and she dreaded taking the paper home for her parents' signatures. She knew they would be disappointed.

Even though she hadn't studied, Lauren was shocked when her test came back with a big fat D.

When she showed the test to her parents, Lauren's mom asked her if she was having trouble in history class. Lauren explained that she had less time to study because of basketball practice and play rehearsal. Her parents told her that she would have to drop one of her extracurricular activities. They said they were proud of her for trying to be involved, but schoolwork had to come first.

Lauren was really torn. She was already committed to her basketball team and to the play. Either way, she'd be letting some people down. She tried arguing with her parents, but they insisted.

"Besides," her mother pointed out, "you've already let someone down."

Talk About It

- **Who has Lauren already let down?**
- **Have you ever had to choose between two activities? How did you make your decision?**
- **Have you ever thought you could slack off and still do well? What happened?**

When Lauren thought about it, she understood what her mother meant. Not only had she let her parents down, but more importantly, she had let herself down. She knew she needed good grades because she wanted to get into a good college someday. And as long as she was doing both of her activities, she wasn't able to give her best effort to either one. So, one of her activities had to go. But which one?

Lauren loved basketball. She had been playing for years, and this was her chance to play for her school and eventually make varsity. She was a really good player, and the team needed her. On the other hand, the play opened in only three weeks. She knew it would be almost impossible for them to find someone to memorize all her lines and play her part. When she told her parents that she chose to stay in the school play and drop basketball, they were surprised. They told Lauren they were proud of her choice.

Talk About It

- Why do you think Lauren chose the school play over basketball?

- What would you have picked if you were in Lauren's position?

- Have you ever had to make a decision in which you'd be letting someone down either way? How did you handle it?

Lauren made the mistake of taking on too many activities at one time. Although she thought she could handle them all, her school-work ended up suffering. There are only so many hours in a day, and priority needs to be given to school. It's fine to be involved in other activities, as long as you have enough time to go around. How you do in school will affect your future. School is your job for now, so do it well.

Part of the reason Lauren took on so much is that she loved the feeling that came with accomplishment. But by getting involved in too many activities, she actually ended up disappointing herself. If you find yourself in Lauren's position, identify one or two interests that are most meaningful to you. That way, you can put in enough time and energy to do your best at those things. More importantly, you'll be able to fully enjoy your participation.

Like the girls in these chapters, you will find that many of the lessons that you learn in school are actually life lessons. Learning to set priorities now will help you create balance in your life later on, as you juggle work and play, friends and family, and other priorities. You will get the most out of life at every stage if you think about what is most important to you and make your commitments accordingly.

Get Healthy

1. When choosing activities, consider how much of a time commitment they require. Think about what you might have to give up, such as time with friends.

2. Don't let activities you care less about eat up your time or create a conflict with something else that's a priority.

3. Talk to your parents or an adult you trust when you feel you've taken on more than you can handle.

4. If an activity begins to interfere with schoolwork, consider whether it is really the right choice for you.

The Last Word from Tina

Sometimes it's a fine line between trying your best and taking on more than you can handle. Students who want to participate in extracurricular activities should choose one or two interests that they enjoy the most, instead of trying to participate in everything available. If your schoolwork starts to suffer, you should consider cutting back. If you focus on a few favorite activities, you'll be more likely to succeed at everything you try, not to mention enjoy yourself along the way.

3

The Slacker

While some kids try to do too much, others tend to slack off at school. Why do perfectly capable students become underachievers? Well, there are several reasons. Maybe they don't care about grades, don't like school, or have other interests they'd rather pursue. Some girls work hard and get low marks anyway, so they decide to stop trying. Others might use their lack of effort as an excuse for their failure, telling themselves, "Well, it's not like I tried anyway." Or, they might give in to the pressure to fit in, since studying all the time and acing a test isn't always seen as cool.

Sadly, adolescent girls often criticize each other, especially to make themselves feel better about their own weaknesses. The girls who make fun of good students often are struggling with their own schoolwork. "Only suck-ups get straight As," they think, "and who wants to be a nerd?"

The girls who make fun of good students often are struggling with their own schoolwork.

Read on to find out how Hayley went from being proud to show her parents her report card to purposely blowing a quiz to show off to her friends.

Hayley's Story

Hayley was popular at her school, but she spent most of her time with her two best friends, Kayla and Samantha. At the beginning of the school year, she was excited that the three of them were in the same math class. Hayley always got better grades than most of her friends. She cared about doing well and spent a great deal of time studying. Samantha and Kayla usually got pretty bad grades and made fun of kids who studied all the time. They called them names like "nerd" and "kiss-up." Now that the three girls were in the same class, Hayley tried to keep her grades a secret. She was worried they would think she was a geek.

One afternoon, the teacher handed some graded tests back to the class. It had been a particularly tough exam, but Hayley had spent a week studying and was anxious to see her grade. When the teacher finally reached her, Hayley was thrilled to see she got a 91 percent, but her happiness was short-lived. Kayla, whose score was only 63, caught a glimpse of Hayley's grade. She threw her own test into her desk and grabbed Hayley's away from her. Then she snickered as she held up Hayley's paper and yelled out, "Hayley's the new teacher's pet!"

Kayla looked Hayley in the eye and said, "Maybe you should switch seats so you can be closer to the teacher. I bet you'd love that!"

Talk About It

- **Why did Hayley try to hide her grade from her friends? How do you think it felt to be in Hayley's shoes?**

- **Why do you think Kayla acted the way she did?**

- **Has anyone ever made you feel bad for doing well on a test or an assignment? How did you deal with it?**

Hayley's face turned bright red. Kayla was supposed to be her friend, but now she had made fun of her in front of the whole class. She looked across the room to where Samantha was sitting, hoping that she might stand up for her. Samantha was laughing at her with the rest of the class. Hayley was humiliated.

After school she raced home as fast as she could. In the privacy of her own room, Hayley began to cry. She felt betrayed and embarrassed. That night she had trouble sleeping. She worried that her friends would make fun of her the next day, too. They had a math quiz the next morning, and she didn't know how to avoid being made fun of again. She had hoped to keep her grades a secret from her friends, but now she knew they'd be looking for reasons to harass her. Normally she would have spent the evening studying, but instead she watched reruns on television and tried not to think about it.

When Hayley got to school the next morning, she went straight to her desk without talking to Kayla or Samantha. When she began the quiz, Hayley looked over her paper and then snuck a glance at Kayla, who was rolling her eyes at Samantha to show she didn't care. Hayley just wanted everything with her friends to go back to normal. Even though Hayley knew a lot of the answers, she skipped most of the questions.

Talk About It

- Why do you think Hayley chose to bomb the quiz?

- Why do you think Hayley wanted her friends' approval, even after their betrayal?

- Have you ever bombed a test on purpose to fit in? How did you feel about your decision afterwards?

The class got their quizzes back the following morning. Hayley had failed. She showed her quiz to Kayla. "I guess I can't be teacher's pet now," Hayley said, shrugging her shoulders.

"Me neither," Kayla replied, laughing at her own failing mark.

Hayley felt relieved. She knew that she and Kayla were friends again. The more she thought about it, though, the more she began to feel disappointed in herself. Now

Even though Hayley knew a lot of the answers, she skipped most of the questions.

that she had the failing mark on her record, she started to think it wasn't worth failing to impress her friends.

Hayley confronted Kayla during lunch. She walked up to her and asked why she'd embarrassed her in front of the class the day before.

"I thought we were friends," Hayley said. "I'm not a teacher's pet. I just studied."

"Fine, whatever," answered Kayla.

Frustrated, Hayley turned to walk away.

Kayla called after her, "Sorry, Hayley. I don't know why I did that. It was stupid."

"It's okay," said Hayley. She was still angry, but she figured she'd forgive her friend in time.

Talk About It

- What do you think about the way Hayley handled the situation? Do you think she and Kayla will continue to be friends?

- Why did Hayley say it was okay when it really wasn't? Would you let Kayla off the hook?

- Have you ever given up friendships with people who were putting you down or holding you back?

Studying to do well in class is the same as practicing your tennis swing for a match or your cartwheel for a competition. Accomplishing something feels good, especially if you worked hard for it. I encourage girls like Hayley to take pride in their academic achievements, rather than hide them.

Kids who put down good grades and think slacking off is cool are really insecure about their own abilities to succeed. If fitting in means you have to downplay your abilities and talents, then you are in the wrong group. Define your own way to be cool. It's cool to be on the honor roll or the dean's list. It's cool to win second place in the science fair. And it's definitely cool to have hard work pay off. What's not cool? Not being yourself.

If you have to dumb down to fit in, then you are not being yourself. If you can't be yourself with your friends, then they are not really your friends. Someone in Hayley's situation might consider hanging out with girls who value doing well in school and walking away from less supportive friendships. True friends are happy for each other's successes. They should cheer you on, not pull you down.

Get Healthy

1. Stand up for yourself. If your friends criticize you for doing well, they are not true friends.

2. Consider what you are losing. Think about whether it's worth letting your grades slide to get along with a friend who puts you down.

3. Try making friends with other students who care about their schoolwork.

4. Get involved in activities with other kids who value being smart and doing well. Try joining groups such as the math club, Future Problem Solvers, or the debate team.

The Last Word from Tina

No one wins if you sacrifice your grades just to fit in. Bombing tests won't make the person making fun of you feel any better about their low marks. More importantly, you end up cheating yourself out of the opportunity to live up to your true potential and the confidence that comes with achievement. Doing well in school helps you succeed in the long run and opens up possibilities that the "cool" kids may never have.

4

The
Mess

Some girls' lockers contain orderly rows of textbooks, labeled folders, and notebooks. These girls can always find their assignments and show up prepared for class. Others face a useless jumble of old notes, handouts, and last week's lunch bag. They might find themselves scrambling to grab the right textbook before the bell rings, getting to the classroom only to see the teacher passing something out. "Wait, that test was today?" Uh-oh.

When it comes to school, some girls have a hard time getting organized. Even though they may be smart and capable, not having a good routine can interfere with their abilities to do well. Junior high means more teachers and more classes, and some kids struggle to meet the beefed-up demands. They may also have poor note-taking skills or sloppy habits, or they may just be plain forgetful. If that sounds like you, a little organization

Junior high means more teachers and more classes, and some kids struggle to meet the beefed-up demands.

can go a long way toward cleaning up your act.

Kim is one girl whose messiness prevented her from doing as well as she could at school. Read on to find out how she dealt with the frustration caused by disorganization.

Kim's Story

Throughout elementary school, Kim was a good student. When she entered junior high for seventh grade, she was really excited. Kim liked that the students changed classrooms for different subjects and had their own lockers. She liked the topics her classes were studying, and the extra responsibilities that came with her new school made her feel grown up. But within the first month, Kim began to have problems keeping up. Her classes were not only more advanced, they were longer. Her teachers' lesson plans were more complicated and required a lot of note taking. No one had ever taught her how to take good notes. Even though she paid attention in class, she couldn't tell which parts she needed to write down. Later, she had trouble making sense of her own notes, so she rarely used them to study. Instead, she tried to rely on her memory.

Talk About It

- **Why do you think it was so hard for Kim to take useful notes?**

- **Have you ever had trouble focusing in class or taking notes? How did you deal with it?**

- **Do you think it was a good idea for Kim to rely on her memory? What would you suggest she do?**

She had so many assignments, textbooks, and subjects now, Kim had trouble remembering everything. She often forgot to bring home the books that she needed for a homework assignment or to study for a test. At school the next day, she would ask one of her classmates what the homework was and then rush through it before the bell rang, but she never managed to finish in time. Test days often came as a surprise, and she'd find herself scrambling to cram. When she started getting low grades, she felt frustrated.

> **She had so many assignments, textbooks, and subjects now, Kim had trouble remembering everything.**

Talk About It

- Why do you think Kim felt frustrated? Was it just the bad grades or something else, too?

- Do you ever forget to bring your schoolwork home? Why do you think this happens? What do you do about it?

- What suggestions would you give Kim?

When Kim did bring her books home to do her homework, it seemed to take forever just to get organized. Even though she was supposed to keep all the notes for her classes in separate binders, she usually just wrote them in whichever one she grabbed first because she felt her notes were useless anyway.

Every time she sat down to do her homework, she would have to flip through a bunch of books to find the pages where she had written down the assignment. By the time she started the actual work, she felt tired and annoyed. She would finish it as fast as she could and throw her books and papers on the floor before she went to bed.

In the mornings, Kim was always in a rush to get to school. She'd gather up her books, but sometimes she forgot one or two. On a few occasions, Kim forgot the binders she'd put her homework in. She got no credit for the late assignments, or she lost points for turning them in late.

As time passed, Kim's grades got worse, and she struggled more and more to keep up. It felt like everything was spinning out of control. She knew she was falling behind in a bunch of her classes but didn't know how to fix it. Kim felt powerless and just wanted to give up.

Talk About It

- Why didn't Kim bother to put her work in separate binders?

- Why did Kim feel annoyed when she did her homework? Why would she throw her books on the floor afterward?

- Have you ever been in Kim's shoes? How did you feel and what did you do?

Then one day, Kim's history teacher, Mrs. Johnson, pulled her aside after class. "I'm confused by you, Kim," Mrs. Johnson said. "Sometimes your work is great, and other times it's as if you didn't even show up to class, even though I know you were here. What's going on?"

Embarrassed, Kim looked down at her shoes. Then she confessed to Mrs. Johnson how overwhelmed she felt, how she had no idea how to take notes, and how she couldn't keep track of seven classes worth of assignments. "I just feel buried by everything," Kim

explained. "Everyone else is keeping up, but I'm a mess."

She expected Mrs. Johnson to lecture her, but instead the teacher nodded her head in understanding.

Talk About It

- Why did Kim feel like everything was out of control? Why did she feel powerless?

- Why was Kim having such a hard time getting organized?

- Have you ever felt like things were out of control? How did you deal with it?

"I thought it might be something like that," Mrs. Johnson said, "so I pulled some information on study skills for you. I keep it on file because I find so many students reach this level without ever learning this stuff."

The next day, while the rest of the class was working on a group project, Mrs. Johnson let Kim go down to the guidance center. There, a counselor gave her some tips on taking notes and organizing her assignments. Kim left the meeting feeling more confident and in control. Plus, she knew she could go back for more help any time she needed it.

Being organized is the key to juggling all the different notes, assignments, and handouts for each class in the upper grades. Like Kim, many students struggle with note taking. Taking useful notes is an important skill that every student should learn. Talk to a teacher or a guidance counselor to see if special help or tutoring is available at your school.

Some helpful hints on taking notes include:

- Use a different color binder or notebook for each class.

- Use a separate page for each new set of notes. Write the date at the top of the page.

- Don't try to write down everything your teacher says. Pick out key information such as important facts, dates, and concepts. Try underlining main ideas so that they stand out later.

Get Healthy

1. Develop routines.

    a) Set aside time for homework each day.

    b) When you finish each assignment, put it in that subject's binder or folder and stick it in your backpack. Keep doing this until all your homework is done.

c) Close your backpack and put it by the door so you won't forget it in the morning.

2. Bring a student planner or an agenda book to class to write down homework assignments and other activities.

3. If you tend to forget to bring home the right books, bring them all home each night.

4. If note taking is a real problem for you, find a friend who is willing to share her notes. You still have to pay attention, but you might find that you learn more if you worry less about what to write down.

The Last Word from Tina

Once you fall behind at school, it can feel impossible to get it together. Not knowing how to get organized can make girls feel frustrated and hopeless. Introducing a few simple techniques can help you stay focused and manage your workload. These activities start with setting up routines and writing down important information where it will be easy to find later. Don't give up! Even when it seems hopeless, it's possible to get organized and gain control over the situation.

5

The Shy Girl

Shyness can be very hard to overcome. Girls who feel nervous about speaking in front of others may have trouble with class participation. They may feel put on the spot or embarrassed when the teacher calls on them. Just about everyone fears public speaking, but if you're already shy, an oral presentation is about as intimidating as it gets. These girls want to avoid being the center of attention at all costs. Anxiety caused by shyness can even cause panic-like symptoms.

The constant nervousness that shy people experience interferes with their ability to concentrate on schoolwork. How do you focus on the lesson when you're so busy dreading the next time the teacher calls your name?

Jada is one girl who had a very difficult time coping with her shyness. Read her story to see how it affected her in school.

Jada's Story

Jada had always been shy. She hated speaking out in class and never raised her hand to answer questions. She was uncomfortable having the whole class listen to her. Plus, she worried about giving the wrong answer.

Anxiety caused by shyness can even cause panic-like symptoms.

The thought of everyone looking at her terrified Jada so much that she felt distracted when she knew her teacher was about to ask someone to answer a question. She always tried to get a seat at the back of the classroom, hoping she would go unnoticed.

Talk About It

- **Why was Jada uncomfortable answering questions in front of the class?**

- **Why did the idea of having to speak in class make Jada feel distracted?**

- **Has speaking in class ever made you nervous? How did you deal with it?**

One morning Jada's science teacher called on her to answer a question. Jada felt panicky. She couldn't stand being put on the spot. She could feel her body shake in fear and hoped that no one else would notice. She answered the question quietly.

"Can you repeat that please, Jada? Louder, so we can all hear you," said her teacher. Jada gulped and forced herself to answer again.

"Sorry, one more time please," replied her teacher, urging her to speak up.

Jada's ears felt hot. She knew her face must have turned red. She wanted to sink into her seat and disappear. She forced her answer out one last time, and it must have satisfied her teacher because she moved on to a new question. It took a long time for Jada to feel calm again. She felt so much dread and embarrassment that she had trouble listening to the rest of the lesson. Just before class ended, Jada's teacher announced that the class was going to start a new project and give oral presentations next Monday. Jada felt like it was the worst assignment she could possibly get.

Talk About It

- Has being called on in class ever made you feel embarrassed?

- Have you ever been worried about giving a presentation? How did it go?

The following weekend, Jada prepared her project. She studied the material and made notes for what she would say on note cards. Even though Jada was prepared on paper, she had no idea how she would get through the actual presentation.

By Monday morning, Jada's nerves made her feel nauseous. As she walked to science class, she hoped that there would be a substitute that day or a surprise assembly. To her disappointment, class went on as planned. Her teacher started calling out names from the student list. Three students presented their projects. Jada couldn't hear anything her classmates were saying. All she could think about was that her name would be called soon and that she would have to get up there, in front of everyone. When Jada's name was called, she grabbed her note cards and walked to the front of the class. Her hands were already beginning to sweat.

Once she saw all her classmates looking at her, she could feel her face going red again. Quietly and with a shaky voice, Jada read the information on her cards as quickly as possible and scurried back to her seat.

Once Jada saw all her classmates looking at her, she could feel her face going red again.

The whole presentation was a blur. She didn't even know if she read her notes in the right order. Once seated, Jada tried to stop her body from shaking and steady her hands. She felt even worse than she had the previous week. She couldn't get herself to calm down, even though she kept telling herself that the presentation was over. She watched as some of the other kids presented and wondered how it was so easy for them.

Talk About It

- **Why was Jada having trouble concentrating on the other students' presentations? Has nervousness ever affected your concentration in school?**

- **Do you think the other students really had as easy a time as Jada thought they did? Why didn't they seem as nervous as Jada felt?**

- **What advice would you give to Jada?**

Ask Dr. Vicki

Fear of public speaking is quite common. However, some cases are more extreme than others. Exceptionally shy girls like Jada often feel overwhelmed when they have to speak in front of the class. Panic or anxiety can decrease concentration levels and even affect how well students do in school. Since speaking in front of others is a necessary skill for later in life, it is important for girls like Jada to learn coping techniques that will help ease their anxiety.

Get Healthy

1. Take slow, deep breaths. Breathe in through your nose and fill your lungs all the way. Then let all the air go, breathing out through your mouth. Sending oxygen to the brain has a calming effect.

2. When you are afraid, it's because your mind is telling you that you should be nervous. Try sending yourself some reassuring messages, such as "I can do this" or "I know the material."

create an image in your mind of standing up and giving your talk successfully. Even athletes do this to gain confidence. They see themselves skiing down the hill or running in first place, etc. It works for them and can work for you, too.

- Think about circumstances in which you don't feel shy. Do you feel more confident around your family? Do you feel relaxed when you're with your friends? Think about how you might apply this confidence in class.

- Practice giving your presentation to someone you feel comfortable with first, such as a friend.

- During the actual presentation, pretend that you are talking to someone you are at ease with, rather than a classroom of students.

The Last Word from Tina

Even though it may feel like shyness is difficult to overcome, the good news is that many people conquer it. In most cases, shyness decreases as we get older. Practice helps speed the process. The more a shy girl participates in class and gives presentations, the easier it becomes. As girls who feel shy become more used to speaking up, it feels more natural

6

The New Girl

Being the new girl is something we all experience at some time in our lives. Some girls experience this when they transfer schools. Others may be new to an activity they have joined outside school, such as a dance class or a sports team.

Being new can be especially difficult for girls who have to switch schools. Adjusting to an unfamiliar environment and being surrounded by new people is a lot to take on. A girl who is new may struggle to fit in among friends who have known each other for a long time. If the experience makes her feel like an outsider, she may feel a lack of confidence and have trouble making friends.

Madison experienced what it was like to be the new girl when she switched schools. Here's her story.

Madison's Story

Madison was an only child who lived with her mother. In the summer before seventh grade, her mom transferred jobs. They moved to a new city, and Madison had to switch schools. At her old school, Madison was friends with girls she had known since first and second grade. She and her friends seemed to have everything in common. They liked the same music and movies and had similar tastes in clothes.

When Madison moved, everything changed. The girls at her new school dressed differently and shared inside jokes that she didn't understand. Even though approaching new people made her nervous, she really wanted to make new friends. So the first week of school, Madison tried to talk to a group of three girls in one of her classes. She overheard Stacey, Kelly, and Amanda talking about music one afternoon and tried to join in on the conversation. Madison and her old friends listened to pop and dance music. She mentioned one of her favorite bands to the girls.

Amanda scowled at Madison. "No one listens to them. What, are you from a different planet?"

> When Madison moved, everything changed. The girls at her new school dressed differently and shared inside jokes that she didn't understand.

The girls giggled. It turned out they listened to hip-hop. Stacey said pop music was for kids. Amanda turned her back to Madison and continued the conversation as if Madison wasn't even there. Madison felt embarrassed by Amanda's reaction and angry that the girls shut her out. She thought about the incident all afternoon.

Talk About It

- **Why do you think the girls shut Madison out of the conversation?**

- **Has anyone ever shut you out of a conversation? How did you feel?**

- **Have you ever had a hard time fitting in somewhere? How did you try to break the ice with new people?**

That weekend, Madison went to the mall with her mom and bought a hip-hop CD. She went home and listened to her new album. She kind of liked it. It wasn't that different from some of the dance music she had. Later that evening, Madison sent a text to Brianna, one of her old friends. Madison told her about the new CD. Brianna sent a text back saying that she didn't like hip-hop. Madison told her she hadn't liked it before, either. But once she listened to it, she changed her mind.

The next week, Madison tried talking to Amanda again. She told her she bought one of the CDs that she'd heard her friends talking about.

"It was actually pretty cool," Madison said.

"Yeah, whatever," Amanda replied, as she rejoined her friends.

Madison felt frustrated. She hated her new school because she felt lonely and out of place. It seemed like nothing Madison tried was making things any easier, so she stopped trying to make new friends altogether.

Talk About It

- **Why do you think Madison bought the CD that the girls at her new school liked?**

- **Has meeting new people ever opened your eyes to something new that you otherwise wouldn't have tried? What was it?**

- **Is Amanda someone Madison should try to be friends with?**

Madison wished she had never moved. The only thing she actually liked about her new school was art class. She was a good painter, so when her teacher announced an upcoming art show, she was really excited. The students were allowed to paint or draw anything they wanted to submit to the show at the end of the semester. The art room would be transformed into the showroom. Madison had a great idea for a painting. She worked on the project for weeks, and by the time it was done, she felt like she had accomplished her best work. When she turned it in, her teacher complimented her on her painting.

During the show, students filed into the art room and scattered to look at different projects. Madison noticed that Amanda, Stacey, and Kelly were standing in a corner, laughing at someone's work. She started to feel nervous as the girls moved toward her painting. Madison was worried they would make fun of it, too, and she didn't want to deal with those girls again.

When the girls walked up to Madison's project, Kelly whispered something to Amanda. Madison felt her hands begin to sweat. She wondered if they were going to embarrass her again. The girls continued to whisper to each other as Melanie, a girl in Madison's art class, approached her.

Madison felt her hands begin to sweat. She wondered if they were going to embarrass her again.

"How did you learn to do that?" Melanie asked. "It's really good."

Madison was taken by surprise. "Oh, just practice mostly. I paint a lot at home."

"It's really cool. I'm really bad at painting. I did a drawing for my project," said Melanie. "Do you want to see it?"

"Sure!" Madison replied.

As Madison began to walk away, Amanda commented that she liked the painting, too.

Madison replied with a brief "whatever" as she followed Melanie to her project.

Talk About It

- Have you ever been the new girl? How did it feel?

- If you have been the new girl, what helped you make the transition?

- What advice would you give Madison?

Ask Dr. Vicki

It's normal to feel unsure of yourself when you're new someplace and trying to make friends. Just because Madison had a bad experience with a few girls doesn't mean everyone would have acted so rudely. When trying to fit in at a new school, it can be fun to find out what the trends are, the way Madison did with hip-hop music. But, it is very important not to make changes that are not true to who you are. If some people reject you, look for others who have more common interests. Don't give up! If some people don't like you, tell yourself it's their loss. Those girls missed an opportunity to get to know Madison, and they realized it too late. By then, Madison had found someone truly interested in her, and she didn't have to change a thing.

Get Healthy

1. Recognize that being the new girl is temporary; you won't always feel that way. It just takes time to figure out how to fit into a new place while still being true to yourself.

2. Try involving yourself in an activity that lets you express who you are.

3. If making friends doesn't work right away, don't get discouraged. Try talking to different people at your school. You may find someone you click with.

4. It's okay to try something new, like listening to a new band or participating in a new activity. Don't change who you are, but stay open to new possibilities.

The Last Word from Tina

It is normal to feel like an outsider for a while when you are put into a new environment. Switching schools usually means having to adjust to some unfamiliar things. Trying new things is a positive way to expand your horizons, even if it doesn't always make you fit in. Being ourselves and allowing our uniqueness to shine through is the true key to making friends. In most cases, the new girl will find her place at her new school in time. Keep in mind that not everyone is a good friend match, so don't let negative experiences stop you from branching out to meet other kids and make friends.

7

The Target

eing bullied is one of the most uncomfortable experiences of any stage of school. Bullying is not just limited to violence. It may take the form of name-calling or spreading rumors. No matter what form it takes, bullying is a serious offense. It victimizes girls and leaves them feeling scared, upset, or even humiliated.

Most often, girls who are being bullied have a difficult time standing up for themselves because they are outnumbered. If the bullies threaten them, these girls also may be afraid to tell someone about what's going on. They may feel that taking action will lead to even more bullying because they will be labeled a "tattletale."

In some cases, girls participate in bullying because they are afraid of becoming targets themselves. Megan found herself on both sides of the situation, and neither was pleasant. Read on to find out how Megan reacted as a victim and as a potential bully.

Megan's Story

Megan and her older brother went to the same school until she started sixth grade and he moved up to junior high. Megan didn't really have any close friends at school. A group of girls in her class made fun of her because she was kind of a loner. Chelsea was an older girl in Megan's class who had been held back a grade. She was usually

No matter what form it takes, bullying is a serious offense.

the one who started making fun of Megan, and she always pressured her friends to join in. It seemed like everyone always did what Chelsea told them to do.

Back in fifth grade, Megan turned to her brother when the girls bothered her outside of class. Whenever Chelsea saw Megan with her brother, she kept her distance. But this year was different. Megan was alone. She dreaded running into Chelsea at lunchtime or while she was walking home from school.

One afternoon after school, Chelsea's friends cornered Megan. Megan tried to walk toward the parking lot to avoid them, but Chelsea walked straight into her and shoved her to the ground.

"Get out of my way, loser!" Chelsea yelled as she pushed Megan.

Talk About It

- Why did Chelsea and her friends pick on Megan?

- How do you think it made Megan feel?

- Have you ever been picked on by other girls your age? What happened?

Megan was too scared to say anything. She tried to get up, but Chelsea and her friends circled around her and kept pushing her down again. They laughed at Megan as she struggled to get away from them. When the girls saw a teacher walk through the parking lot, they let Megan go and walked away. Megan stood up and picked her school bag up off the ground. She walked home as fast as she could, praying that she wouldn't run into Chelsea again. She hated that this kept happening but didn't know how to stop it.

Megan was too scared to say anything. She tried to get up, but Chelsea and her friends circled around her and kept pushing her down again.

Talk About It

- Why did Chelsea's friends corner Megan and push her to the ground?

- Why do you think Megan was too scared to speak up?

- Should Megan have told the nearby teacher what was happening? Why do you think she didn't?

The next morning, Megan tried to convince her mom that she was sick because she couldn't bear the thought of having to face the girls at school. Her mom made her go anyway. That day the girls ganged up on Megan again. Over the next few weeks they kept confronting her; they called her names, hit her, and threw things at her. Megan felt helpless and ashamed. She didn't know what to do.

Talk About It

- **Why do you think Megan pretended to be sick instead of telling her mom what had happened?**
- **Why did Megan feel ashamed when the girls harassed her?**
- **What advice would you give Megan?**

In October, a new girl named Alex was put in Megan's class. She seemed shy and mostly kept to herself. Megan overheard Chelsea talking about the new girl. She told her friends that Alex probably had to switch schools because everyone hated her so much at her old school.

"Just look at her," Chelsea said. "As if anyone would be friends with her."

During lunch period, Megan saw Chelsea and her friends talking to Alex. She knew they were harassing her. She could hear them laughing the same way they did when they ganged up on her. Megan walked by them unnoticed and felt relieved that they weren't focusing on her anymore. A few hours later, one of Chelsea's friends walked up to Megan in the hall and told her that they were going to "get" Alex after school.

"You should come see," Chelsea's friend said. "It's going to be hilarious."

Megan wasn't sure what to think. She wondered if they were setting her up so that they could attack her again. Then she thought maybe if she went along with them, she wouldn't have to deal with them bugging her anymore.

Talk About It

- Why did Chelsea and her friends want to "get" the new girl? Why would they tell Megan?
- What should Megan do with the information?

After school, Megan walked into the schoolyard and saw the girls walking behind Alex. One of them walked past Megan, grabbed her by the arm, and led her over to the scene. Chelsea started to push Alex the way she'd pushed Megan. The girl beside Megan nudged her and laughed.

"What a loser," the girl said to Megan.

Megan thought about joining in. She knew it would make her life easier, but every time she looked at Alex, she saw herself. She knew Alex was terrified of what was happening to her.

Megan called out, "Leave her alone!"

Chelsea turned to Megan and said, "Why would I leave her alone? She's such a loser. Just like you. Stay out of it."

"You don't even know her," said Megan. "Leave her alone."

As soon as the words came out of Megan's mouth, she knew that she wasn't just talking about Alex. She was talking about herself.

Talk About It

- What prompted Megan to stand up to Chelsea? In what way was Megan really talking about herself when she did this?

- Have you ever been asked to join in on bullying someone? What did you do?

- Have you ever confronted a bully? What happened?

Ask Dr. Vicki

Being bullied is really scary. Girls like Megan are often afraid to stand up for themselves because they are outnumbered. Targets of bullies often feel defenseless. However, finding the strength to stand up to bullies is usually what puts an end to the situation.

Bullies pick on other girls to make themselves feel better. They use fear to get attention or to make themselves feel more powerful. Standing up to bullies usually works because if they think you are no longer afraid of them, they will no longer feel as though they have power over you.

Often, girls join in on bullying someone just to try to fit in and take the focus off themselves. But like Megan, they usually feel terrible about it. Megan realized that she could speak up for Alex and herself at the same time. She also knew that she was no longer alone; she and Alex would be allies.

Some people might advise you to "just ignore it." Although they are trying to be helpful, it may seem like they don't understand. Help them see the situation through your eyes, not theirs. That's what communication is all about.

Get Healthy

1. Speak up. Bullies pick on girls who they feel won't stand up for themselves.

2. Speak out. If someone you know is being bullied, stand up for them.

3. Tell someone. Tell a teacher, a guidance counselor, or the principal what's going on.

4. Remember that you are not alone. You may not be the only one who is targeted by the person who is bullying you. If you know other girls going through the same experience, try sharing your feelings with them and see what they have to say about the situation. Stick together and stand up for each other. Bullies like to pick on one person at a time; they don't usually take on a group.

The Last Word from Tina

No one deserves to be bullied. Unfortunately, bullying is common at school. The best way to deal with it is to stand up for yourself. When bullies feel like they no longer pose a threat, they lose interest in attacking.

If you feel like standing up for yourself is not an option, ask for help. Help can come from the school faculty or from other girls who also are being harassed. Bullies who act as a group maintain their power through numbers; you can do the same.

8

The Nerd

Nerd. Dork. Loser. Nobody wants those labels, but that doesn't stop young girls from using them on each other. Why would they be so mean? During adolescence, some girls tend to reject girls who struggle to fit in because of the way they dress or their awkwardness in social situations.

Being given a negative label can lead to girls developing poor self-esteem. It is easy for these girls to be influenced by what other girls say about them. Rejection may make them experience self-doubt. They may feel isolated from their peers and be reluctant to try to make friends based on a fear of further rejection.

Alison was someone who was classified as a "nerd" by the girls at her school because she dressed differently and didn't get involved in the same activities. Feeling like an outcast made her doubt her ability to make friends. Take a look at Alison's story to see how she dealt with the label.

Alison's Story

Alison was the younger of two girls who lived alone with their father. When her parents got divorced, Alison was in fifth grade, and her sister was in ninth grade. Alison's mom moved to a new city across the country. Alison talked to her mom on the phone every week but only got to see her during spring break and summer. It was hard not having her mom around. She knew her dad tried his best, but there were things she couldn't talk to him about because she thought he wouldn't understand.

While other girls Alison's age went shopping for new clothes for the upcoming school year, Alison was forced to wear her sister's hand-me-downs.

Even though her dad worked two jobs, it seemed like their family was always short on money. While other girls Alison's age went shopping for new clothes for the upcoming school year, Alison was forced to wear her sister's hand-me-downs. She felt embarrassed about wearing old clothes. By the time Alison got them, they were really out of style.

When she started junior high, Alison felt like an outcast. Other girls in her class spent time together at the mall. They bought fashion magazines and wore the latest trends in clothes and makeup. They went to salons to get expensive haircuts and highlights. Alison knew her family couldn't afford all the new things her friends had. Her dad didn't let her wear makeup, even though everyone else was allowed to. Alison had some friends in elementary school, but even they were getting into fashion and makeup, so she didn't feel that she fit in with them anymore, either.

Over time, Alison became a loner at school. Some girls called her a nerd because they thought she dressed weird, and she always seemed to be by herself. Boys in her classes ignored her completely. No one ever chose to sit beside her in class or picked her for group assignments. She began to wonder if her classmates were right. She didn't feel like she was different, but if everyone else thought she was a nerd, then maybe she was.

Talk About It

- **How much does someone's appearance really say about who they are?**

- **Has someone ever said anything about you that made you doubt or dislike yourself?**

- **How do you think Alison felt about being labeled a "nerd"? Have you ever been given a label? How well did it describe you?**

Alison's science teacher assigned her to work on a project with three other girls. Alison felt nervous about participating because she didn't know the other girls very well, and the project would involve getting together outside of school. She was really worried that they weren't going to like her.

When the girls met up to work together, Alison was surprised that she got along with them really well. One of the girls, Tabitha, loved a movie that happened to be Alison's favorite. The girls talked and joked together.

The girls talked and joked together. Alison really felt like she was part of the group, instead of an outsider.

Alison really felt like she was part of the group, instead of an outsider. When the assignment was finished, she felt sad that she no longer had a reason to hang out with Tabitha and the other girls.

Talk About It

- Why was Alison so surprised that she got along with the girls in her project group?

- Why do you think that Alison had never made the effort to make friends with her classmates before?

- What do you think she will do differently now?

During the school week, the girls Alison had worked with talked to her in class, but the next Saturday Alison was stuck at home alone again. She'd had so much fun working with the girls in her project group that she wished she could just call and ask them to do something. She had Tabitha's cell number and e-mail address. Still, Alison felt hesitant to contact her. She worried that maybe the girls were only being nice to her so they could get through the assignment. She was afraid that if she tried to make friends with them, they would reject her, so she didn't do anything.

Talk About It

- Why do you think Alison assumed the girls didn't really like her?

- What advice would you give to Alison to help boost her confidence?

- Have you ever been in a situation where you weren't sure that people liked you? What did you do?

On Sunday afternoon, Alison thought about the situation again. She knew that if she didn't even try, she would definitely be stuck by herself. She took a deep breath as she got online and e-mailed Tabitha.

Having a fear of being rejected by their peers can cause some girls to put up walls or isolate themselves from other girls at their school. However, socializing with classmates and meeting new people is an important part of adolescence. Making friends provides girls with essential social skills that they will use in the future, not to mention someone to hang with on the weekend.

Alison lost her confidence because she let what others say about her affect what she thought of herself. When she let her personality shine through during the group project, she discovered that she did have things in common with other girls.

Get Healthy

1. Take risks and meet new people, even when you feel scared. Focus on what you might gain by reaching out to new friends, rather than worrying about possible negative results.

2. See situations that involve new people as opportunities to make new friends. Study groups and extracurricular activities offer common ground.

3. Don't let what other people say about you define who you are. You are the only one who can truly define yourself.

4. If you really want to be more in style, but your family is on a limited budget, shop at thrift shops, discount stores, and consignment shops. You'll find much lower prices on clothes, accessories, or shoes that could help update your wardrobe.

The Last Word from Tina

A label is never an accurate description of who someone is. Unfortunately, once someone has been given a label at school, it may be hard for her to be seen otherwise. When a girl is given a negative label and others start to treat her poorly or ignore her because of it, she may start to believe what the other girls are saying about her. It's important to remember that you know yourself best, so don't let what others say change how you feel about yourself.

9

The
Nothing

dolescence is a time when girls are just beginning to discover who they are. As girls start becoming more conscious of their own identities, they may seek out ways to define themselves and others around them by classifying or labeling themselves and their peers. Cliques often begin to form around these labels. When girls are part of a group, others might prejudge them instead of really getting to know them. Many labels or classifications form out of a single defining characteristic. Girls may be pigeonholed based on how they dress, what music they listen to, how much they care about academics, or what their social status is.

On the other hand, those who don't fit into a given mold and can't seem to find a group that suits them may have a harder time making friends. These girls may feel left out, ignored, or like they have no identity.

Jess knows what that feels like. Read on to find out how she dealt with not fitting in anywhere.

Jess's Story

Jess had never considered herself popular. At her junior high it seemed like everyone was divided into groups. There was a group of girls known as the Populars—everyone wanted to be like them and be liked by them. Then there were the Jocks—that one was pretty self-explanatory. Others were known as Emos,

Girls may be pigeonholed based on how they dress, what music they listen to, how much they care about academics, or what their social status is.

Goths, or Skaters because of the type of music they listened to, how they acted, and the way they dressed. The girls who did really well in school, joined a lot of activities, and stayed out of trouble were called Preps, while girls who didn't spend much time socializing were called Nerds.

It seemed like all the groups had formed out of the blue. In elementary school, a few kids had been more popular than the others or excelled at sports, but no one had cared as much about labels. Now, for the most part, everyone socialized only with his or her own group. Jess had a hard time trying to figure out which group she belonged in. Everyone wanted to be a Popular, so Jess tried hanging out in the courtyard with them, laughing at their jokes and trying to act cool.

After a while, Jess started feeling as though she didn't fit in anywhere.

No one paid her any attention. Shortly after, she started to wear all black to fit in with the Goths, but they just called her a "wannabe." She knew she wasn't a Jock, and with her grades, no one would ever call her a Prep. She liked to have fun and went to school activities, unlike the Nerds, who never went to anything. After a while, Jess started feeling as though she didn't fit in anywhere. At lunchtime she had nowhere to sit because the other girls sat with their own groups. Sitting alone in the cafeteria, Jess looked around. What she really felt like was a Nothing.

Talk About It

- Why wasn't Jess part of one of the groups at her school?

- Why do people break off into cliques? Do you think knowing what group someone belongs to is a good way to know what they are like?

- What groups are present at your school? Do you consider yourself to be part of a clique?

As the school year continued, Jess found it difficult to make friends because she wasn't really part of anything. Girls talked to her in class, but no one ever invited her to do anything outside of school.

Talk About It

- Why didn't anyone invite Jess to hang out outside of school?

- How do you think Jess felt about not being included in anything?

- What would you do in her position?

Jess's classmates treated her like she was a Nothing because she didn't fit in anywhere. She started to feel like she was invisible, like no one even cared she existed. She felt confused and began to feel like she didn't know who she was. She knew what things she liked. She loved dancing. She liked funny movies and thought she had a good sense of humor. Most of all, Jess loved animals and was signed up to start horseback riding lessons in the spring. Still, none of her interests seemed to help her find a place to belong.

Talk About It

- **What made Jess feel invisible? Have you ever felt this way?**

- **Why did Jess feel like she was a Nothing?**

- **Did the fact that Jess didn't fit in at her school mean she was a Nothing?**

At the beginning of April, Jess was about to start her first horseback-riding class. She wondered if she was going to have trouble fitting in with the other girls in her riding class, too. When she arrived at her lesson, Jess saw Amber, one of the Goth girls from her school. She was really surprised to see someone like that taking horseback riding lessons and wearing riding clothes instead of all black.

Amber walked up to her and said hi. She asked Jess if she was new to horseback riding.

"Yeah, this is my first lesson," Jess explained. "Is it your first class?" Jess asked her.

"Oh . . . no," Amber laughed. "This is my third year. I just never tell anyone at school I take lessons because they think I'm Goth."

"You're not?"

"Not really. I like the music, but my friends are more into it than I am. I guess I just started dressing that way because it makes it easier to hang out with them. They'd make fun of me if they knew I rode horses."

Talk About It

- **Why was Jess so surprised to see Amber at her horseback-riding lesson?**

- **Has the fact that someone belonged to a group ever caused you to make assumptions about who she is?**

- **What do you think about Amber's choice to pretend to be Goth?**

Being part of a group can feel good because you have friends and common interests, but faking who you are the way Amber did means you aren't being true to yourself. She thought she had to hide who she really was in order to have friends.

Like Jess, some girls try to make themselves fit into a group without success. Girls who don't really belong to any group may actually feel like a Nothing and start to wonder what's wrong with them. They may really start to question who they are and how they want to be. This is a time to be true to who you are, not to try to conform in ways that don't feel right for you.

Not fitting in with a group usually means that you have a lot going for you and a variety of interests. In this case, trying to fit in with a clique would limit your interests and talents. As you pursue those different aspects of yourself, you may find that you end up with several groups of friends.

Get Healthy

. Think about how you define who you are. For example, are you smart, caring, funny, or outgoing? Do you have special talents or

2. Try to get to know other girls for who they really are, rather than making assumptions based on their cliques. Ask girls questions about their interests.

3. If you are feeling isolated, consider other ways to meet new friends, such as participating in extracurricular activities or joining classes or teams outside school.

4. Talk to someone about how you are feeling. Sharing your feelings with someone you trust can make you feel less alone.

The Last Word from Tina

When girls judge each other by their cliques, they miss the big picture. Belonging to a group or an inner circle at school doesn't really define who someone is. It may focus on one aspect, such as being good at sports, but it ignores all the other interests and talents that make each girl an individual. Just because you don't fit in with a group at school doesn't mean you are a Nothing. You are a whole lot of things. Your thoughts, your personality, and your likes and dislikes make up the real you, not who you hang out with.

10

The Slow Reader

Having a learning disability has nothing to do with how smart someone is. For whatever reason, some students learn differently from others. It doesn't mean they can't learn or won't learn. It means they need to be taught in ways that work best for them. Learning disabilities can affect skills such as reading and writing, math comprehension, memorization, organization, and attention. Letting an adult know if you are having trouble learning and getting support in the form of tutors and/or different learning aids is the key to success in such a case. Getting the right help is important to progressing forward.

Kaitlyn was a student whose learning disability caused her to have more trouble with reading than her classmates. Her story shows how getting help can turn things around for girls who are struggling in school.

Kaitlyn's Story

Kaitlyn had been having a hard time keeping up in school for as long as she could remember. She read at a lower grade level than the other kids in her class. In elementary school, she was tested by the school psychologist and found to have a learning disability in

Kaitlyn had been having a hard time keeping up in school for as long as she could remember.

reading. This caused her to read very slowly and have trouble understanding what she read. After her problem was discovered, the school wrote up an Individual Educational Plan (IEP) that provided her with special tutoring in the resource room, shortened her assignments, and allowed her to have extra time to take tests and do assignments whenever she requested it.

When she started junior high, she made new friends who didn't know that she had a problem with reading. She was worried that they would think she was dumb if they knew she had to get extra help. So, she never asked to go to the resource room for help and never asked her teacher for extra time, even when she couldn't finish a test by the end of the period. Even though she struggled with the amount of homework, she didn't want anyone to know that she had any problems.

Without a tutor, she had a hard time keeping up with schoolwork, and her marks started to drop rapidly. It seemed to take her forever to get her work done and to finish tests. When her teachers explained a homework assignment, she was able to follow what was going on, but every time she read through her textbooks or her teachers' handouts, she couldn't make sense of what she was reading.

Talk About It

- Should Kaitlyn have kept her reading difficulty to herself, or should she have told her friends the truth?

- Do you think it was worth it for Kaitlyn to opt out of tutoring to keep her reading problem a secret from her friends?

- Have you ever had difficulty with something at school and kept it a secret?

At home, she would read a chapter three or four times before she even started to grasp its meaning. When Kaitlyn was assigned book reports in English

class, she wasn't able to finish the whole book on time, even though she read the assigned books each evening and on weekends.

Kaitlyn was actually good at math. She even understood geometry, which other students found difficult. When it came to word problems, though, she just didn't get it. She read each sentence slowly but could never understand what the problem was asking her to figure out.

One morning, Kaitlyn's history teacher had the class take turns reading a paragraph from the textbook out loud. When it was Kaitlyn's turn, she asked if she could pass, but her teacher said that everyone had to take a turn. As she read the paragraph slowly, she mixed up the order of some of the words and pronounced some words incorrectly. She could feel the class staring at her impatiently and felt embarrassed and ashamed.

Talk About It

- Why did Kaitlyn ask her teacher to pass on her when the class was asked to read out loud?

- How could Kaitlyn have prevented an embarrassing situation like this?

- What advice would you have for Kaitlyn?

At night, Kaitlyn began to get more and more frustrated when she tried to do her homework. It felt like she could never get anywhere with it. She thought it wasn't fair that she had such a hard time with her schoolwork, while it

As she read the paragraph slowly, she mixed up the order of some of the words and pronounced some words incorrectly.

seemed to come so easily to other girls. She wished she could be like everybody else, but it all seemed too impossibly difficult.

In November, Kaitlyn's math teacher assigned a take-home test on a Friday afternoon, to be completed over the weekend. The exam was mostly word problems. On Saturday afternoon, Kaitlyn sat at the kitchen table and looked over the test. She couldn't understand the questions. She tried to look up examples in her math book, but the samples didn't make sense, either. After reading the test for more than an hour, Kaitlyn gave up. She knew she could have asked one of her parents for help, but she didn't bother. On Monday afternoon, she had nothing to hand in when her teacher collected the tests from the other students. When her teacher asked where her test was, she said she didn't do it. She was asked to stay after class.

Talk About It

- What do you think Kaitlyn meant when she wished she could be "like everyone else"?
- Why did Kaitlyn give up on doing her assignment instead of asking someone for help?
- Have you ever skipped an assignment that you needed help on? What happened when it was time to turn in your work?

Kaitlyn's math teacher spoke to her privately. She asked her why she didn't do the assigned work.

Kaitlyn explained, "I tried to do it, but the questions didn't make any sense. I read over them a bunch of times, but I don't know what they're asking."

Kaitlyn's teacher went over the questions with her one at a time. When she explained them, they made sense to her, but as soon as she tried to read one on her own again she was lost. When her teacher noticed that she still had a hard time understanding the questions, she suggested that she get some extra help developing her reading.

Kaitlyn told her about her learning disability. She explained that she used to get special tutoring and extra time in elementary school, but that she hadn't asked for help this year because she didn't want everyone to think that she was dumb.

"You're not stupid, Kaitlyn," said her teacher. "You understand the work when it's explained to you. I didn't even know you had an IEP. All your teachers should have been told so that we can help you the best we can. You need some help improving your reading comprehension skills to pass this class, and you are definitely entitled to have the services listed in your IEP."

Kaitlyn realized that if she didn't get help, she might not pass the year. That would be worse than her friends finding out she had a learning disability. She agreed to talk to her guidance counselor so that all her teachers could be told about her IEP. Once she had permission to go to the resource room, Kaitlyn started working with the special tutor. With help, she was able to keep up with her homework. It still took her longer than her classmates to get her work done, but with

the extra time and shortened assignments, her grades were finally improving. Kaitlyn still didn't like feeling different from her classmates, but she understood that she had to accept help to keep up. She realized that even though her process of learning was different, in the long run she was able to do as well as anyone else.

Ask Dr. Vicki

Having a learning disability can be embarrassing to many students. They are afraid that their classmates will think they are stupid. Usually intelligence is not the problem; rather, these students just need to be taught in a way that works best for them. With extra help, modifications, or special instruction, most students can do as well as their peers. However, if you do not take advantage of the assistance offered, you probably will not do as well, and your grades will suffer, which could be even more embarrassing.

No one is perfect. We all have our shortcomings, and we all need help now and then. Being willing to ask for help in order to succeed shows bravery and is actually an important skill to use throughout your life. Reaching out for help when needed doesn't make you look dumb. It's actually a very smart thing to do!

Get Healthy

- If you have an IEP, every teacher should know about it and provide you with whatever modifications are listed for you. If the teacher does not cooperate, tell your guidance counselor or your parents. An IEP must be followed by law. Your parent or guardian can request a new IEP meeting to review what assistance you need.

2. If you are having trouble keeping up with your work, it doesn't necessarily mean that you have a learning disability. Tell a teacher or guidance counselor what is going on. You may need a little extra help, or you may be evaluated to see if there is a specific learning problem. Schools can usually provide extra help to students who need it.

3. See what additional learning aids might be available. A selection of books, recordings, and Web sites are available to those who have learning difficulties. You might also consider getting a tutor to assist you with catching up on your workload or to help you stay on track.

4. Recognize that there is no shame in asking for help. Feel confident about the fact that you are taking charge of your situation.

The Last Word from Tina

There is no quick fix for girls who have learning disabilities. But with the right help, girls who have learning disabilities can find ways to do better in school, go on to college, and be very successful in life. Accepting extra help allows you to take charge of your situation and overcome the obstacles presented by learning disabilities.

A Second Look

As you have now read, all kinds of challenges come with being a student. No one is good at everything. Discovering your strengths and recognizing your weaknesses are essential skills for growing into yourself and becoming aware of who you are.

By now, you may have already considered what parts of school you excel at and what things don't come as easily to you. Having this knowledge puts you on the right track to success. Now you can set goals for yourself and brainstorm ways to meet the challenges ahead.

Just remember, when problems arise that are more than you can handle on your own, don't be afraid to ask for help. The school environment is designed to help students meet their educational goals and to make school life run a little more smoothly. Teachers and guidance counselors are there to assist you.

Once you've identified an area that could use some improvement, don't give up! Whether your ambitions include getting better grades, getting organized, making friends, or something else entirely, remember that success comes with time and determination.

XOXO,
Tina

Pay It Forward

Remember, a healthful life is about balance. Now that you know how to walk that path, pay it forward to a friend or even to yourself! Remember the Get Healthy tips throughout this book, and then take these steps to get healthy and get going.

- Find ways to help you relax before a big test or other stressful event. Try taking deep breaths, counting backward from ten, or listening to your favorite music beforehand.

- Prioritize your commitments. Make sure you're devoting yourself to activities that are truly important to you, and not letting activities you care less about eat up your time.

- Think about who your friends are and whether they deserve your friendship. If your friends criticize you for doing well, they are not true friends. Try to hang out with people who like you for who you are and support your efforts to succeed.

- If you have a problem you can't handle alone, don't be ashamed to tell an adult. Whether you're facing a bully or coping with a learning disability, help is available. All you have to do is ask!

- Think about what situations you feel confident in, such as when you're with your family or friends. What are you good at, and what do you like about yourself? Try to channel that confidence into situations where you feel less sure.

- Develop routines that will help you stay on top of things. Organize your notes and homework assignments in separate binders and notebooks for each subject, so you always know where to find them later. Keep track of your to-do lists in a student planner or an agenda book.

- Try something new, whether it's joining an activity or listening to a different kind of music. You might discover something you didn't know about yourself, and even meet some interesting people in the process!

- Don't let what other people say about you define who you are. You are the only one who can truly define yourself.

Additional Resources

Selected Bibliography

Philp, Raleigh. *Engaging Tweens and Teens: A Brain-Compatible Approach to Reaching Middle and High School Students*. Thousand Oaks, CA: Corwin Press, 2006.

Stabiner, Karen. *Reclaiming Our Daughters: What Parenting a Preteen Taught Me About Real Girls*. Emeryville, CA: Seal Press, 2007.

Zager, Karen. *The Inside Story on Teen Girls: Experts Answer Parents' Questions*. Washington, DC: Magination Press, 2002.

Further Reading

Cummings, Rhoda Woods, et. al. *The Survival Guide for Teens with LD (Learning Differences)*. Minneapolis, MN: Free Spirit Publishing, 1993.

Erlbach, Arlene. *Middle School Survival Guide*. New York, NY: Walker & Company, 2003.

Espeland, Pamela. *Life Lists for Teens: Tips, Steps, Hints, and How-Tos for Growing Up, Getting Along, Learning, and Having Fun*. Minneapolis, MN: Free Spirit Publishing, 2003.

Ford, Amanda. *Be True to Yourself: A Daily Guide for Teenage Girls*. Berkeley, CA: Conari Press, 2000.

Mosatche, Harriet. *Too Young for This, Too Old for That! Your Survival Guide for the Middle-School Years*. Minneapolis, MN: Free Spirit Publishing, 2000.

Web Sites

To learn more about school survival skills, visit ABDO Publishing Company on the World Wide Web at **www.abdopublishing.com**. Web sites about school survival skills are featured on our Book Links page. These links are routinely monitored and updated to provide the most current information possible.

For More Information

For more information on this subject, contact or visit the following organizations.

Learning Disabilities Association of America

4156 Library Road, Pittsburgh, PA, 15234-1349
412-341-1515
www.ldanatl.org
This organization provides support, information, and resources for people with learning disabilities, as well as their parents, teachers, and professionals who work with them.

Toastmasters International Youth Leadership Program

P.O. Box 9052, Mission Viejo, CA, 92690-9052
949-858-1207
www.toastmasters.org/MembersMemberExperience/
SatellitePrograms_1/YouthLeadership.aspx
Offered through Toastmasters International and its local chapters, this program was created to help young people improve their communication, public speaking, and leadership skills.

Glossary

anxiety
A feeling of worry or fear.

assumptions
Statements or ideas that someone supposes to be true without checking.

clique
A small group of people who are very friendly with each other and do not easily accept others into their group.

concentration
The act of focusing one's thoughts and attentions on something.

confidence
A strong belief in one's own abilities.

emphasis
Importance given to something.

harassing
Pestering or annoying someone.

isolated
Kept alone or apart from other people.

learning disability
Difficulty learning a basic skill, such as reading, because of a physical condition, such as dyslexia.

outcast
Someone who is not accepted by other people.

pigeonholed
Categorized in a way that fails to reflect the complete person.

priority
Something that is more important or more urgent than other things.

sacrifice
To give up something important or enjoyable for a good reason.

trend
The latest style or preference.

victimize
To pick someone out for unfair treatment.

Index

About the Author

Tina R. Gagliardi is a freelance journalist, as well as an author of fiction and nonfiction books for young readers. Her work has appeared in *LUSH Magazine*, *East of the City*, and *Regina Weese*, among others. She works and resides in Toronto, Ontario.

Photo Credits

SW Productions/Jupiterimages/AP Images, 13; Robert Payne/iStockphoto, 17; Jacom Stephens/iStockphoto, 22; Kenneth C. Zirkel/iStockphoto, 27; Willie B. Thomas/iStockphoto, 33, 45; Ned Frisk Photography/Jupiterimages/AP Images, 43, 99; Liza McCorkle/iStockphoto, 50; Paul Kline/iStockphoto, 52; Image Source/AP Images, 59; Chris Schmidt/iStockphoto, 61; Rob Melnychuk/Jupiterimages/AP Images, 63; Robert Churchill/iStockphoto, 69; Peter Finnie/iStockphoto, 73; Image Source/Getty Images, 78; Barbara Sauder/iStockphoto, 87; iStockphoto, 95